D1266436

Adventures with Collage

ADVENTURES WITH COLLAGE

by JAN BEANEY

With 50 photographs by Alan Wysman

FREDERICK WARNE & CO. INC.
NEW YORK AND LONDON

First published by
KAYE & WARD LIMITED
194–200 Bishopsgate, London EC2
1970

Copyright © 1970 Kaye & Ward Ltd
As 'Fun with Collage'
First United States Publication 1970
Reprinted 1971
Frederick Warne & Co. Inc.
Library of Congress Catalog Card Number 79–128406

Printed in Great Britain by
Fletcher & Son Ltd, Norwich

CONTENTS

All black and white photographs in this book were taken using a 5″ × 4″ monorail camera with Kodak Plus X film and color filters when necessary to maintain tonal separation

Collage by Pamela Thorpe. Various materials used, including nets, threads and painted wood shavings

INTRODUCTION

The word *collage* is derived from the French verb *coller* meaning to stick. A collage is a picture or pattern built up wholly or partly from pieces of paper, cloth and/or other materials stuck onto a background.

This work is mainly taught instead of painting, but usually tries to imitate it, which is a mistake as the very nature of the medium is not suitable for this. Materials can be cheap 'junk', such as papers, fabrics etc., and can be collected at home or at school. Working in collage can improve your sense of pattern, color and texture, your sense of inventiveness or creativity, your deftness and experience of working with a wide range of materials. It can be used to support the learning and understanding of other subjects in the school curriculum and can easily lead on to designs for embroidery, decorative and three-dimensional work; or it can be treated as a work of art in its own right.

Collage can be approached in a number of special ways—such as a fine art form as used by Picasso or Braque—but the emphasis in this book will be on extending the colorful, decorative and textural qualities which are within the composition range and experience of young people. Each aspect which should be considered when creating a collage picture will be dealt with in turn, so that a wide approach to design and imaginative use of materials can be achieved. Once the learner has gained confidence in working in this medium, then greater freedom and creativity develop.

Design incorporating metallised and matt papers

Various sized washers and nuts assembled into a pattern

BASIC MATERIALS NEEDED FOR COLLAGE

Scissors
Tweezers
Spatula
Small jar for glue
Background material–strong paper, wall lining paper, plain or corrugated card
Charcoal, chalk
Old newspapers for covering work tables
A collection of varying types of plain colored papers
All types of decorative 'junk'–foil, bottle tops, beads, buttons, seeds, fabrics, threads, plastics etc.
Cellophane tape
Rubber cement
White casein glue, e.g. 'Elmer's'

The background paper for your collage picture should be strong and firm so that it will take a fair amount of glue plus the weight of the materials stuck to it without buckling or puckering.

Design showing the use of a variety of papers and acetate

Decorative head. Many types of paper used, including tissue, wallpaper offcuts and crêpe paper. Additional decoration includes beads, curtain rings, gold cord, d'oyleys and thumb tack tops

10

ADHESIVES

It is most important to use the right glue for a particular purpose.

Rubber cement is a rubber-based adhesive and is more manageable if you apply it by finger, or, in some instances, by spatula. It is useful for glueing all papers, card and some fabrics and has the important advantage whereby, if a mistake in glueing is made, the piece of paper can be lifted and stuck in another place. All traces of the glue will then peel off when rubbed, leaving a clean surface. This adhesive is especially useful when first experimenting with basic pattern shapes at the start of a collage picture.

A casein glue such as 'Elmer's' is the other glue recommended for this work. It will glue most surfaces together, is clear drying and is very strong. It should be applied with a large, soft brush and used sparingly in small drops. If too thick, add water.

Unlike rubber cement once this glue has dried it is really permanent, and there are two points to remember here. Firstly, if you do use a brush to apply the adhesive, clean it immediately after use, as if it is left to dry the glue will harden and render the brush useless. Secondly, do remember to wipe the rim of the bottle or tube before replacing the cap, otherwise it will adhere firmly. If this should happen, soak the container in a bowl of water and with average luck the cap should loosen.

Although there are many brands of glue on the market, most are designed for specific purposes. Many liquid ones are sufficient for sticking papers but not strong enough for holding the heavier decoration you may wish to use. You will be confused and disappointed if, after all your efforts and creativity, your work comes apart within hours of completion or after a short time in a centrally-heated atmosphere.

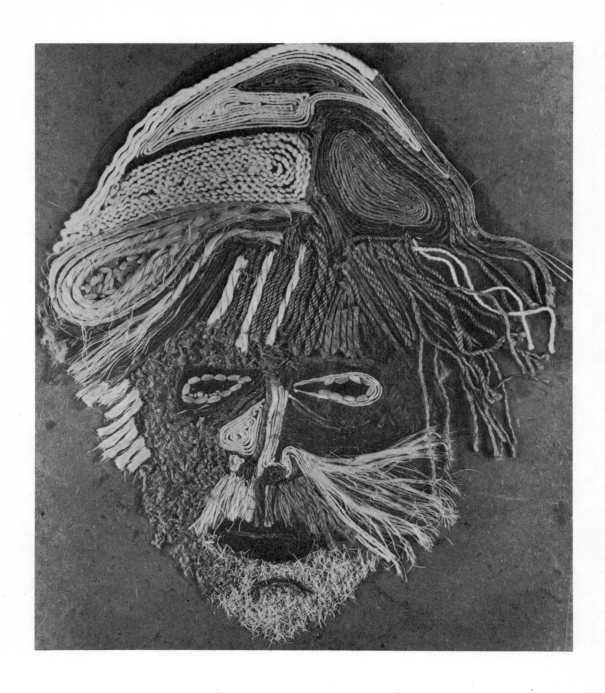

Design made from a variety of string and threads, both unravelled, frayed and cut into tiny fragments

12

SOME GLUEING HINTS

When you paste tissue paper, some pieces can be glued on the back and then placed in position on your picture, but if you are covering a large area, it is wiser for the background to be glued in sections and the smaller tissue pieces placed onto it.

If you are decorating with coils of paper, cylinders, strips etc., glue the chosen area on the background and position the pieces into the glue.

When using thread, always glue the background where you wish it to be laid rather than attempt to glue the actual thread. Place it firmly into the glue and maneuver into the desired pattern or order.

Firm or closely woven fabrics can be glued on the back but loosely woven materials, especially net, are best placed onto a glued surface.

Single beads, seeds or very small materials can be placed onto adhesive already dotted on the background surface. Tweezers will probably help to place the seed etc. exactly into the required position.

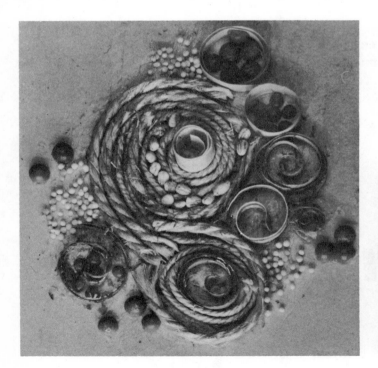

Texture motif made from string, wood shavings, split peas, lentils, pearl barley etc.

All-over texture made from coils of metallised paper

13

PATTERNS AND PAPERS

This section deals with making patterns in a variety of papers and is usually the first stage to consider when creating a collage picture.

Begin by collecting all types of papers, such as tissue, crêpe, wallpaper offcuts, matt, shiny and embossed papers, in as many colors as possible. Plain or textured papers are best as the patterned ones can distract attention from your own design.

Regardless of whether your picture portrays a realistic or an abstract subject, you must always consider most carefully not only the actual shapes you are cutting and planning to glue to the background, but also the spaces that will form additional patterns between the shapes. To help you gain experience of this problem, you could attempt some simple exercises to make you more aware of the importance of background spaces.

Firstly, if you cut and arrange a few identical white paper shapes onto a sheet of dark colored paper, leaving only small spaces between each shape, you will notice that the background, which forms another pattern, links all the parts into one decoration. If, however, the paper shapes are positioned too far apart, they will be seen in isolation and not as a whole design. A general rule is to keep the background spaces less in area than the main pattern shapes.

Secondly, try making several patterns of two or more identical shapes in two types of paper in the colors of your choice.

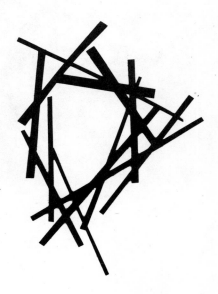

Cut paper pattern by Susan Tindley—10 years

Pattern showing development of background spaces, using shiny and matt papers. By Susan Tindley—10 years

Cut paper pattern by Joyce Ireland—11 years

The next stage is to give further consideration to the cut paper shapes, the background spaces or both. Simplicity is usually the secret of a successful design, and often you can develop the pattern by cutting paper shapes which echo the basic plan and which can be placed within the existing design. By contrasting types of paper and choosing a limited color scheme, an exciting pattern can be created.

Tissue paper is one which is produced in a wide range of colors and possesses the quality of being semi-transparent, so that if you overlap two or more pieces of varying color, other colors will be made. For example, a yellow tissue placed over red will make orange. New exciting colors can be made by tearing and overlapping several different colored tissues and glueing them onto a background. Add further interest by overlapping a number of layers of tissue in one color only, to discover the range of tones you can achieve.

When you have experimented in this way with tissue paper, cut out some shapes and arrange in a pattern, taking great care to consider the background

Design made by overlapping tissue paper shapes. Wool thread has been coiled to emphasise certain parts

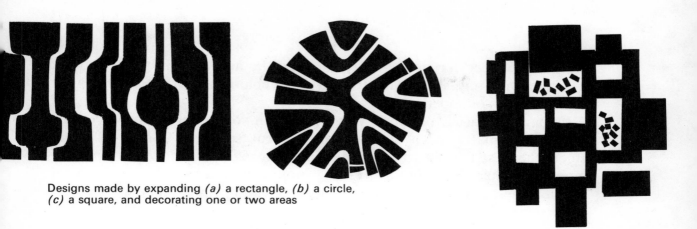

Designs made by expanding *(a)* a rectangle, *(b)* a circle,
(c) a square, and decorating one or two areas

spaces. Create interest by overlapping colors within the pattern. Remember to contrast plain areas with highly decorative parts; do not overdecorate all parts of the design, as it may lose its original character and become confused.

You may find it fun to make a pattern by expanding a certain basic shape, such as a circle or square. Choose a saucer, box or jar etc. as a template (pattern), place it on a piece of paper, draw round the chosen object and cut out. From this cut out pieces of contrasting shape–that is, big, small, fat and thin–and arrange on another sheet of paper in the exact order of cutting. If the shapes are pushed together, they should again form the basic pattern. Then with all these in the right order, leave a small space between each, thus forming a new pattern, and glue into place. Try this exercise using one colored paper for the basic shape and another for the background. On completing

Patterns made by grouping small pieces of paper of varying shape

the design, select one or two interesting smaller areas within the design and decorate with tiny shapes cut from a third colored paper, remembering to vary the types of paper.

If you use a variety of papers you will see that you can also achieve contrast with shiny, matt, rough and semi-transparent surfaces. Choose a limited color scheme so that the varying papers are more effective. Make some patterns based on either circles or squares of various sizes, pasting them one on top of the other, using contrasting colors and cutting away shapes to expose other papers beneath.

Continue to experiment, using your imagination. Cut strips of paper in varying widths to form a pattern made by vertical lines. If you vary the size of the spaces between patterns and overlap in part, you will eventually find a design you like.

Create another pattern by arranging strips of paper of varying dimensions horizontally and vertically. Isolate one or two spaces and decorate with solid blocks of color or tiny scraps of paper.

Add to your collection of papers by looking through some used magazines and tearing out from illustrations or advertisements areas which are plain

Pattern made by arranging strips of paper horizontally and vertically, with one or two spaces enriched by smaller shapes of paper

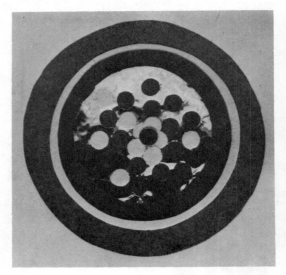

Design based on various sized circles, cut away in part to expose other surfaces. Tissue, matt and highly reflective papers used

18

colored or of textured appearance. You will find many beautiful colors in a wide range of tones, such as sections of sky, a cornfield, the sea, a carpet, a road etc.

The main thing to bear in mind in this section is that it is reasonably easy to achieve the most exciting pattern if attention is paid to the following points:

1. Remember to use a selection of papers.
2. Contrast plain and highly decorative areas.
3. Plan carefully the background shapes so that the design is considered as a whole and not as a number of isolated parts that do not link happily together.

To help increase your awareness of pattern and texture, go out and really look and, if possible, sketch the patterns you will find all around you, such as groups of pebbles, tree bark, a section of layered soil, tiles on a roof, the exotic markings on a butterfly, the pattern on a leaf partially eaten by a caterpillar, and so on.

Butterfly. Basic shape in silver Mylar, encrusted with overlapping tissue shapes, tinfoil, pearls, nuts, washers etc.

TEXTURE

In the first section you have experimented with various types of paper and exploited their particular qualities, such as the semi-transparent appearance of tissue and the reflective effect of shiny papers. By putting the various qualities of paper together, thus letting one enhance the other, you have become concerned with texture. One definition of texture says that it is the degree of openness and closeness in a surface or substance when felt or looked at – for example, cloth, skin or wood of loose, fine or coarse texture.

To make your collages more exciting, you should vary and contrast textures. Having dealt with paper in the flat, you can experiment to see what patterns and textures you can make by using papers in other ways. Besides building patterns with paper shapes by cutting, overlapping and then glueing in place, you can cut paper into thin strips and interweave, roll, pleat, fold, screw into shapes, loop, curl, partly cut and bend in certain directions. Try experimenting and see what interesting results you can achieve.

White construction paper, coiled, curled, looped, folded and bent

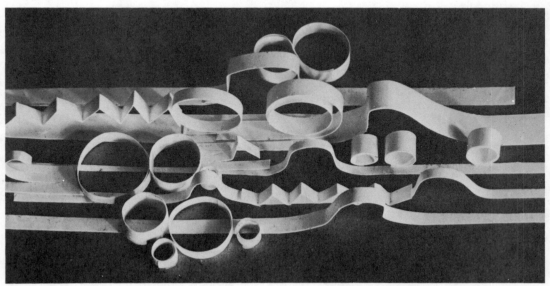

Decorative surfaces can be made with more pliable materials such as aluminium foil, metalised paper, milk bottle and ice-cream carton tops. Play around by rolling, cutting into, bending or molding some or all of these materials.

Using some of the knowledge and experience you have gained since the start of the book, you now probably have a number of ideas for making a picture or pattern. However, if one does not come to mind immediately, perhaps a collage of a planet or giant dream flower might inspire you. How would you imagine the centre of the sun or the surface of the moon or some distant planet? Use what materials you like and feel would be suitable for the particular effect you might want, such as cragginess, rock formation, still, deep, glossy pools, vast wasteland, caves, deep lagoons and dykes, pebbles, fossils and plant life etc.

'Planet' by Peter Bennet—9 years. Variety of materials used, including aluminium foil, milk bottle tops, seeds

If a giant dream flower has more appeal, how large would the petals be? Would they overlap and sport beautiful markings? Would the centre be richly decorated and so on? Make sure you plan the complete design, remembering to contrast heavily textured and plain areas, or you may find that you concentrate on isolated parts of your picture which do not link up when the collage is viewed as a whole. Assemble the main areas in flat paper and then build up from the basic format. From some of the paper layers cut out shapes,

'Dream Flower' by Joyce Ireland—11 years. Opaque, transparent and metallic (mirror-finished) papers used, enriched with split peas and tapioca

revealing other colors and textures beneath. Contrast matt and shiny surfaces and finally enrich with small details.

You could be even more subtle and selective by contrasting textures within certain groupings. For instance, the shiny surface of foil wrapping taken from a cigarette packet is not as bright and reflective as aluminium foil or mirrored acetate. Notice the difference between the matt surface of white construction paper compared with the smoothness of white paper bags used by bakeries and delicatessens.

'Silver Planet' made from silver kid leather, mirror glass, pearls, aluminium foil, ice-cream carton tops, silver braid, cigarette packet foil, silver Mylar

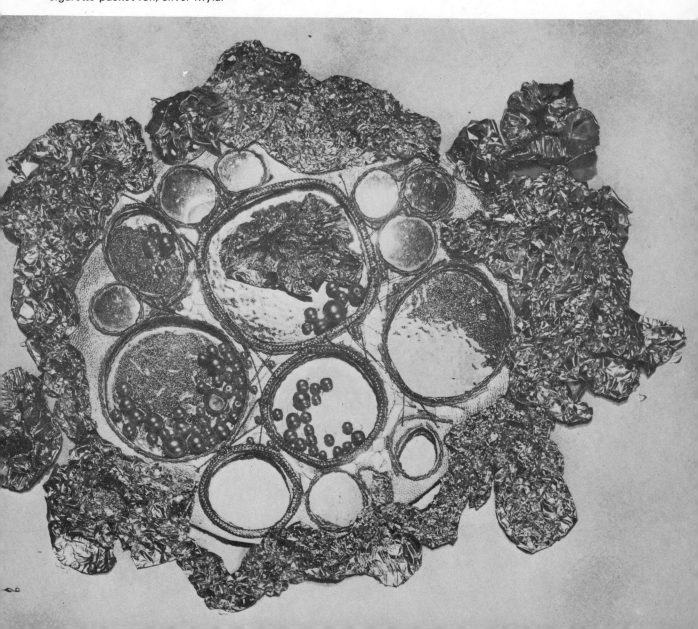

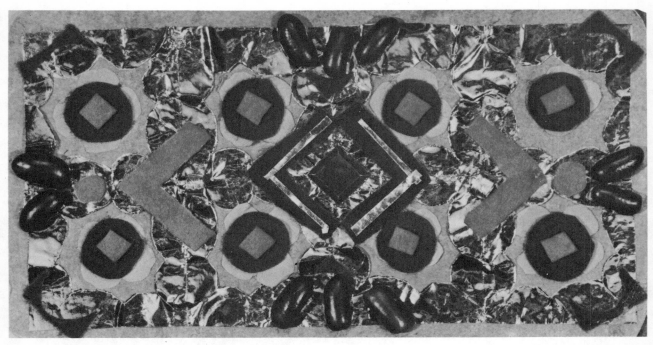

Pattern made with metallised paper, felt pieces and beans

Fish by Susan Ward—10 years. Interwoven string and thread used

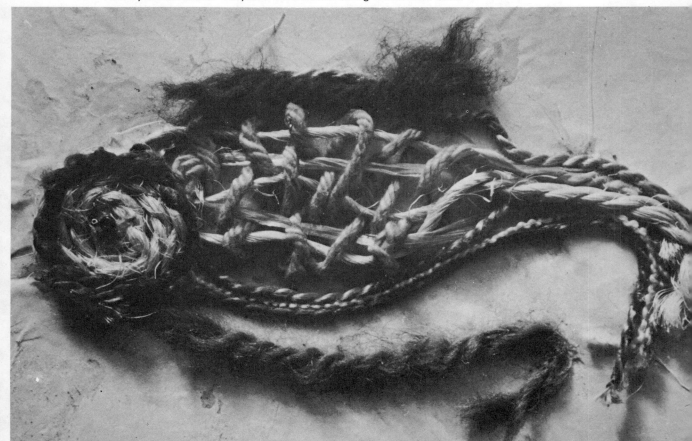

If you make yourself aware of things about you in everyday life, you will soon collect hundreds of exciting types of materials with which to build a collage. A visit to a building site might mean you could be given a collection of wood shavings, various-sized nails, gravel, tiny decorative pebbles; or a factory might spare scrap metal shavings and filings etc. In your own home you may discover decorative pasta shapes, lentils, split peas, used matches, corrugated card, fabrics, string, bird seed and so on. You may be lucky enough to find tiny stones, twigs and seeds in your garden, in the local park or on a visit to the country. All these materials vary in size, quality and color and are ideal for adding to your collage patterns. For convenience, sort your collection and store in boxes and bags.

Start gathering together scraps of fabrics in solid colors and of varying texture. You will probably be able to collect small pieces from your mother or a friend who makes her own clothes. Your collection could consist of floating chiffons, coarse sacking, fine wool, glossy silks and taffetas, rich

Motif designed with pasta wheels, string, wood shavings, split peas, lentils, pearl barley, egg macaroni and tapioca. By Joyce Ireland—11 years

Pattern made with screws, washers and wing nuts

25

velvets, crisp cotton, matt felt and soft leathers. Separate the materials in color groups and store in plastic bags. There are so many exciting fabrics useful for collage and embroidery.

Loosely woven materials which fray readily enable you to create varying patterns, especially where the threads can be easily pulled out of order. This can be done either singly or in groups, holes can be pierced or pulled and threads looped to make fascinating textures. With the closer weaves holes

Felt flaps cut and bent back to form a pattern with applied coils of felt

can be cut and sections partially cut and rolled or bent in various directions. Try obtaining different surfaces by deliberately fraying or unravelling sections of knitting to give a gnarled, uneven effect. You will soon appreciate how exciting and rewarding such experiments in creating textures can become.

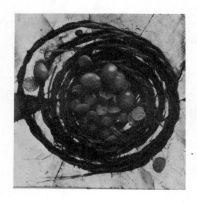

(Left) String, split peas and lentils
(Right) Assorted beads and sequins

In addition, embroidery threads, knitting wools, weaving yarns, rug wools, string and ribbons can be woven, coiled, looped or stitched to form shapes and emphasise and link designs.

If matt fabrics and threads have been used, introduce sparkle with assorted beads and sequins. In order to give greater effect, these should be glued in clusters or shapes rather than used in isolation.

Textures made by looping various threads, including wool, raffia and gold leather strips

DECORATIVE TREATMENT

When collecting ideas and notes for certain subjects from life around you or from books, look carefully for the detail of the existing patterns and decoration. You may be fascinated by the fine intricacies of veins on a leaf, the rich centre of a flower, seashells, the elaborate carving above a door, interweaving branches, the patterns of light and shade, a coiling hairstyle, streamers on a warrior's horse, the translucent wings of a dragonfly; the list is endless. Only you can decide what it is about each subject that appeals to you.

As collage is in general a bold medium needing a bold approach, it seems suitable to exaggerate and give these special features a larger than life interpretation. Simplify or magnify the proportions of the existing shapes so that you have more scope to experiment and decorate. For instance, if the spot patterns on a fish interest you, then increase their size and decrease their number. You may like a particular shape of a certain leaf and the patterns within it, so you could make a tree dressed in a few highly decorated leaves, rather than depict hundreds of small leaves arranged in a realistic way.

A beautifully feathered crest on a bird's head might appeal; therefore enlarge the proportion a little and make it even more grand. The tail feather patterns might be exotically vivid, each with intricate markings. Select for illustration only a few enlarged feathers so that the finer details can be interpreted in a much bolder way.

The main factor is for you to be inspired and to collect ideas. However, as collage is a broad medium, when illustrating by this means do not attempt to imitate exactly a realistic view or a literal interpretation or become confused by proportions, perspective and the like. Allow the color, pattern and shapes to be of prime interest; lessen the importance of some parts and exaggerate the areas that particularly interest you.

'Bird' by Susan Tindley—10 years. Made with tissue papers and enriched with metallised paper, milk bottle tops, seeds and pearl tapioca

Fabric collage—stitched. By Selina Rand—14 years. Shows an
interesting choice of fabric for cloud effects and the body
of the horse

Stylised designs showing
wave effects

Subjects which involve movement can be a challenge and need particularly careful thought to achieve a successful result. For instance, the movement and shape of clouds and smoke should be closely observed before you attempt an interpretation. You will see that smoke moves in a variety of ways; it can coil upward, drift, billow, puff, spiral etc., and from any one of these you can form the basis of a pattern. Try and depict the movement by using thread, cut paper or other materials rather than glueing blobs of cotton wool, which is the usual unimaginative approach to the creation of such an effect. This material is also often misused when illustrating hair or a beard on a decorative head. With a little thought other materials could be used far more imaginatively.

An expanse of water can be presented in a number of ways. Ask yourself if you want it to appear still, rough with 'white horses' or waves rolling and crashing one on another. Decide on the movement suitable for your picture and simplify the shapes.

Stylised designs showing smoke patterns

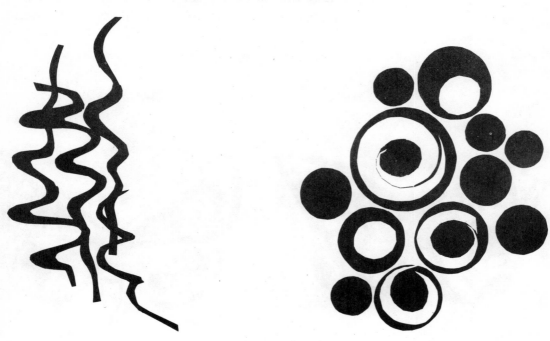

MAKING SMALL COLLAGE PICTURES

Although you may at first feel that the creation of a small collage picture offers less imaginative scope than a larger theme developed with other people, it is the approach to looking at and really seeing the subject that is so important. If you can form the habit of asking yourself questions about things around you so that you look objectively, your powers of observation will improve and consequently your awareness of color, shape, pattern and texture. You will then find it easier to tackle a subject with more definite views. When you have worked through certain stages of your picture and you do not know how to develop it further, if you ask yourself another question or two, fresh ideas will probably come to mind.

The following are a few points to help you to be successful:

1. When starting a picture think carefully about the subject and then choose your color scheme.
2. Sketch the main shapes and outlines only on your background paper, or work directly in cut paper, taking care to consider the background spaces.

3. Build up the larger areas first, in varying types of paper, so that the general design can be seen. Do not concentrate on an isolated part to begin with, as the picture must be developed as a whole.
4. Put in lines developing or linking parts of the design. Emphasise both the inside and outside of the basic shapes.
5. Add smaller pieces of paper or fabric to build up patterns, but leave some plainer areas. Remember to overlap papers or cut shapes away to reveal other surfaces.
6. Continue to develop some areas with interesting textures and details, e.g. seeds, foil, beads etc.

If you wish to make a picture of a fish, for instance, before starting ask yourself several questions. When looking at a fish in an aquarium or photo-

Pattern made with shiny papers, thread, net, beans and beads

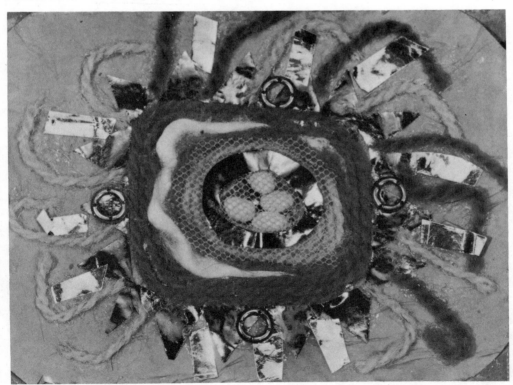

Fish by boy—9 years. Main shape decorated with lumps of glued
tissue paper

Fish by boy—9 years. Made with metallised paper, cellophane
and egg shell fragments

graphed in a book, notice the main body shape and the size and shape of its tail. How does the tail join onto the body? What color is it and is it patterned in any way? How would you describe the main feature of the fish; for example, is it spotty or striped? Does it glisten or is it roughly textured? Has it huge teeth and eyes, or does it sport a vicious or humorous look? Where and in what sort of surroundings does it live? This last point is very important, as it may possibly provide the basis for the design of your collage background, thus creating an immediate atmosphere for your work. Always pay attention to these details when designing pictures of birds, animals and many other subjects. **1690318**

When preparing to plan a picture which incorporates buildings, start by looking at details around you on your way to and from school, while shopping or on some other trip. Make a note of the different shapes of buildings and the variety of chimneys, doors, porches and windows that you can find. You will soon decide which ones attract you and be able to use them as the basis of your collage. Remember to exaggerate or simplify certain features, enhancing

decoration and making the picture more suited to this bold medium. For example, to attempt to make a literal picture of a brick house would take too long. It would be far more exciting to depict fewer bricks and concentrate on interpreting their subtle range of colors or the decorative brickwork which is often found round the edges of doorways, windows and under eaves. Stone houses are extremely decorative, and it would be fairly easy to interpret the various patterns and colors. There are in fact, so many exciting features

Castle by boy—9 years. Various papers used, including tissue and wall-paper scraps

you can observe and build into your design, such as towers, spires, weather cocks, arches, balconies, shutters, carving, ironwork, colored blinds and window boxes.

Although you want a building to be recognisable, there is no need to strive after a very realistic image; and by using the wealth of varied materials collected, you can have great fun and produce an impressive result.

Japanese fish by Japanese girl—8 years. A richly decorative
picture built up by tiny fragments of assorted papers

DEALING WITH LARGE AREAS OF SIMILAR COLOR

When dealing with large areas of similar color within your picture (for instance, an expanse of sky or sea), your task will be made easier and far greater decorative effect will be achieved if this area is broken up. Do not choose one large piece of paper, as most papers, especially tissue, can be difficult to handle; it will easily pucker and crease, or the glue will show through unevenly. Furthermore, a large area of the same color can become boring to work on if approached in the wrong way. Although you may want a plain area to contrast with more decorated parts, it need not lack interest. For example, if you are about to create a blue sky in your picture, choose several pieces of paper in varying shades of blue, rather than one large sheet, so that small shapes can be torn or cut and glued into place, next to one another. To give a more interesting effect, you may prefer to overlap the paper or leave tiny cracks of the background showing through. These suggestions can apply to a number of subjects, such as the large expanse of a long dress, vast fields and hills, paths, roadways and so on.

After cutting or tearing a number of pieces of paper ready to paste on the larger area, do not glue each piece separately, but spread glue over part of the space to be covered and place a dozen or so bits of paper down quickly. This method will enable you to build up the areas far more swiftly and will leave you time to manipulate the more detailed and individual parts. To add further interest, other shapes or textures could be applied to the expanse, but remember to keep within the chosen color range so that the area preserves its unity and does not become over fussy.

GROUP PROJECTS

It can be most enjoyable to make a large picture with a group of people, and this section will help you to organise such a project. After gathering together some friends at home or at school and discussing a subject to illustrate by means of a collage picture or wall frieze, you must first decide how the picture is to be planned. For instance, if figures are to be included, agree on the number and whether they are to be important features. If buildings are to form part of the design, consider the style of architecture, both interior and exterior. Supposing that the scene is to be set outdoors, will it portray a street, a garden or a landscape? Is it to be in summer or winter and so on? Each question must be answered so that everyone in the group knows what the main aims are, even though they will each be free to interpret and design their own contribution.

Having decided these points, it is wise to choose one member of the group to organise and co-ordinate all the tasks, which can be allotted as follows. One person can measure and tape together the background paper, card or fabric, using cellophane tape, then pin or staple it to the chosen display area. Two people can collect the glue, spatulas, scissors and newspapers and arrange the colored papers and other materials in easily accessible parts of the room. The remaining members of the group can collect details from books and magazines about the chosen subject. For example, if the Norman Conquest is to be portrayed, they should find out facts about the scene of the battle, soldiers' armour and the type of horse trappings and banners used in that period. Do remember, however, that these observations are not to be copied exactly but to be used only as a source of inspiration and to form the basis of an engaging picture.

If the old favorite 'Autumn' is the chosen subject, try and give it an original interpretation. Have a long, searching look at the shapes of various trees and their many characteristics. Observe the size, shape and color of the leaves and the type of pattern they make against the sky, in groups on the ground or when caught up in swirls of wind. Notice the texture of tree trunks. Are they smooth, patchy, ridged, gnarled or mossy etc? So often these scenes are depicted by identical squat tree trunks which end abruptly, isolated leaves being stuck here and there without any real consideration.

40

'Tree with a hole' by girl—8 years. Materials are string, corrugated cardboard and various papers, including tissue

'Fireworks' is another popular theme often interpreted in a dull way, perhaps by a few isolated star shapes in pink and green. If you really think about it, you will find that a host of patterns and colors come to mind which could create an exciting basis for a picture. Ask yourself what shapes the clusters of exploding fireworks form and what patterns they make as they fall to the ground. There are so many assorted fireworks in vibrant colors, and some of these form graceful sprays or fan out into exotic forms. Others are like fountains within fountains or form swirling movements and inner movements, such as those made by pinwheels.

Church by boy—9 years. Materials include tissue, paper torn from
magazines, wall-paper offcuts, gold foil from cigarette packets

'Weird machine' by Rory Gibson—10 years. Design worked in
overlapping tissue papers and decorated with pasta wheels and nuts

A story or a poem may give you inspiration or an historical event or a certain type of landscape which you have learned about in your geography lessons. Maybe a nature walk, an outing to the Zoo or a school visit to a city or a farm could suggest other ideas. It can also be great fun making a purely imaginative collage depicting strange creatures, dream flowers, weird machines and so on. There is no limit to the subjects you can use.

Once all the materials, reference notes and sketches have been collected and the background prepared, pause and decide on the next jobs to be allocated. One or two people can sketch the main composition or outlines on the background. Use charcoal or chalk for a large collage and not a lead pencil, as you are likely to become confused by details and not see the collage as a whole or as a bold decorative statement. Stand back and look at your sketches from time to time; it will be easier to see if it is developing the way you desire. Alternatively, it is sometimes a good idea to first assemble the picture in cut paper shapes, and, having arranged these satisfactorily, you can draw round

Picture by Susan Tindley—10 years, and Joyce Ireland—11 years.
Inspired by a nonsense story by Edward Lear and showing a rich variety of papers

them to leave a design on your background. You can use the shapes again afterwards as templates for making up the design in colored papers and textures. This is quite a quick way of building a picture and often avoids confusion and simplifies the arrangement of the picture.

The large or basic shapes usually need to be tackled first, and other smaller items, such as flowers, figures, trees and animals etc., applied afterwards. Some people can cut or tear paper to fill in the larger expanses on the background, such as large buildings, floors, sea and sky. Others can be employed in making individual shapes to stick to the background or they can mass produce petals, leaves, stones etc. Obviously, those people who collected the reference notes should be employed, for example, in creating the detail of gnarled tree trunks, organising chain mail on a knight's armor, making intricate flower centres, elaborately decorated and coiled hairstyles, the pattern of a ploughed field and so on. Whatever the subject, do remember

Collage depicting a river scene with buildings in the background, created by a group of students from Whitelands College of Education from small pieces of colored paper torn from magazines

to build up the basic shapes boldly first in cut paper, then decorate with other colors and textures before adding the final details.

You must bear in mind that this is essentially a team effort, and discussion should take place at each stage.

Sometimes it can be a good idea to limit color but at the same time vary the range of tones within a certain color scheme. For instance, a large field of varying red and orange flowers in a wide range of textures could give a bold and exciting effect, whereas a field of multi-colored flowers in hectic blues, reds, yellows and greens may become a little confused, with each bright color competing against the next. If, on the other hand, you were picturing the court of Henry VIII with all the nobles and their ladies dressed in richly decorated and multi-colored robes, the background walls and floor might be the only 'quiet' areas in toning colors and the means of linking the picture as a whole.

Decorative head by teacher training college student. Various
papers, including metallic and wall-paper scraps, net and string
have been used

FABRIC COLLAGE—GLUED

It is fun making a collection of odd scraps of colored material and various lengths of thread. You can easily create a picture using the fabrics as the basic shapes with the threads linking, outlining and enriching the design.

Solid colored and textured materials of any kind are suitable; the more varied the texture, the more exciting the result. It is advisable to keep to these rather than printed textiles, which can sometimes compete with or distract attention from your own pattern.

Look back at some of the experiments you did in the section dealing with texture. Some parts of your design might be enhanced by frayed materials or loosely woven ones with interesting patterns pulled in them. Cutting holes in materials and pasting other colors and surfaces behind can also give a rich effect.

When you have decided on a subject, you may feel sufficiently confident to cut directly into the fabric for the basic shapes. Alternatively, you can lightly chalk the design on the material before cutting. If you wish to use a really intricate shape, however, it is advisable to draw it first on paper, then cut it out and pin it to the material to be applied. Using the paper shape as a template, cut out your material shape, position it and glue it to the background paper or fabric. If desired, continue by sorting through your collection of textile scraps and decide whether you wish to apply any smaller shapes of material to form a pattern on top of the basic design.

Another idea is to develop the pattern with a variety of threads made, for example, from wool, raffia and metal. If you would like to outline some of the shapes in this way, decide whether to do this within or around them and concentrate on the larger or bolder areas first. You may wish to decorate your picture with stripes, coils, spirals, geometric patterns, loops, interweaving etc., using various types of thick, thin, rough and smooth threads. Pause again and look back to some of the small exercises you created earlier in the book for fresh inspiration. Having used as many of the threads as you wish, finishing details may be added by using beads, buttons and coils of felt. Remember to leave some plain or uncluttered spaces to contrast with the more highly textured parts.

When you have completed several collages by glueing fabrics to the background, you will be ready to move on to the next stage, where the fabrics and threads are stitched into place.

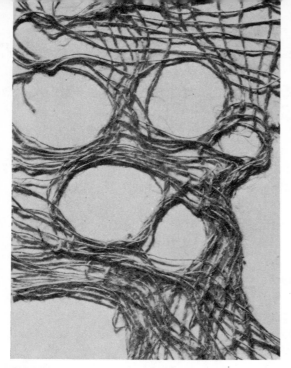

Sculpture scrim—a loosely woven fabric which easily pulls out of order to form exciting patterns

String pulled into interesting shapes

Pattern made from various types of string

'Warrior's Head'. Fabric collage by boy—12 years. Materials used are linen, rep, chiffon and felt

FABRIC COLLAGE—EMBROIDERED

Materials needed:
A selection of fabrics, threads, beads
Fine thread for sewing down fabrics
Scissors, pins, chalk
Assorted needles, including a bead needle and one with a large eye that will
    take thick threads

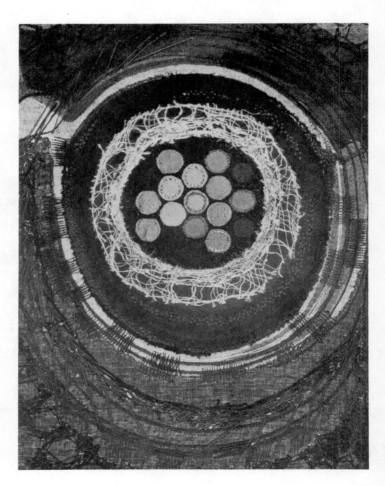

Section 'Underground Cables'
embroidery. Applied sculpture
scrim, felt and other fabrics.
Mainly worked in couching and
straight stitches

(a) STRAIGHT STITCH This is shown as single spaced stitches worked either in a regular or irregular manner. Sometimes the stitches are of varying size

(b) COUCHING Lay a thread along line of design and with another thread tie it down at even intervals with a small stitch in the fabric

(c) SEEDING This simple filling stitch is composed of small straight stitches of equal length placed at random over the surface as shown on the diagram

Select for embroidery a small picture or design from your collection of glued fabric and paper collages. You should usually find that these are suitable for interpretation by this means. Make a tracing of your picture and cut into areas to make paper patterns. Choose a suitably firm background fabric in a color you like and also a variety of materials you wish to apply. Remember to limit your colors but include a wide range of tones and contrast the fabric characteristics as suggested in the last section. Using the paper patterns, cut out the materials. In most cases, the fabric being applied should match the direction of the warp and weft of the background to prevent puckering. To create interest, layer materials in some areas, cut away shapes and possibly use semi-transparent materials such as net. Having completed the cutting, arranging and pinning of the materials to the background, sew into place with a fine thread in matching colors. Acceptable methods are to herringbone stitch all fraying materials and catch stitch non-fraying materials such as felt, net and leather.

Choose interesting yarns to outline or define certain shapes by couching curving lines, tight spirals, loops, crosses and other patterns that will enrich and echo the basic design. There are many methods of using straight stitches and a selection of these will add interest. Buttons, sequins, beads and padded patches can be applied to contrast with the existing materials.

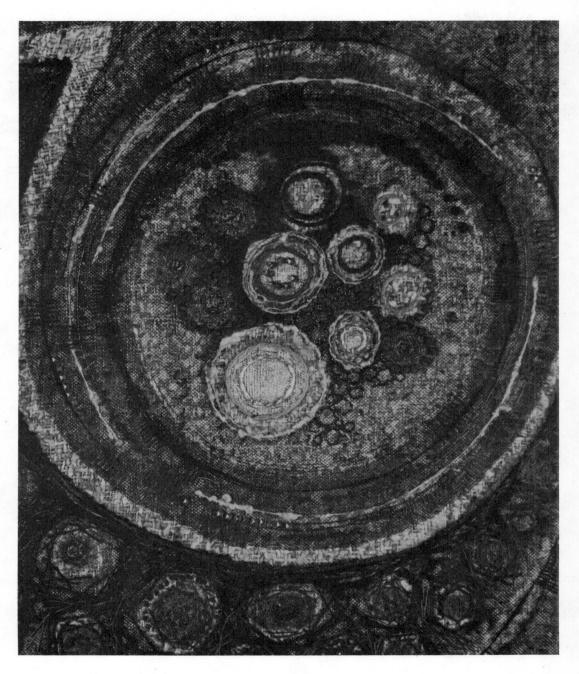

Section from 'African Stone' embroidery. Circular patterns couched
in a variety of threads

52

COLLAGE IN RELIEF

This method of building patterns out from the background is exciting because of two main aspects. Although you still need to consider the design when seen from the front, there is the added interest of a side view; both aspects are equally important, and this is known as collage 'in relief'.

Begin by building some cylinders of different dimensions, grouping them closely together. The shadows that fall one on another will in themselves

Motif made from a painted cake container surrounded by shiny paper, petals and curls. The centre is enriched by beads and sequins

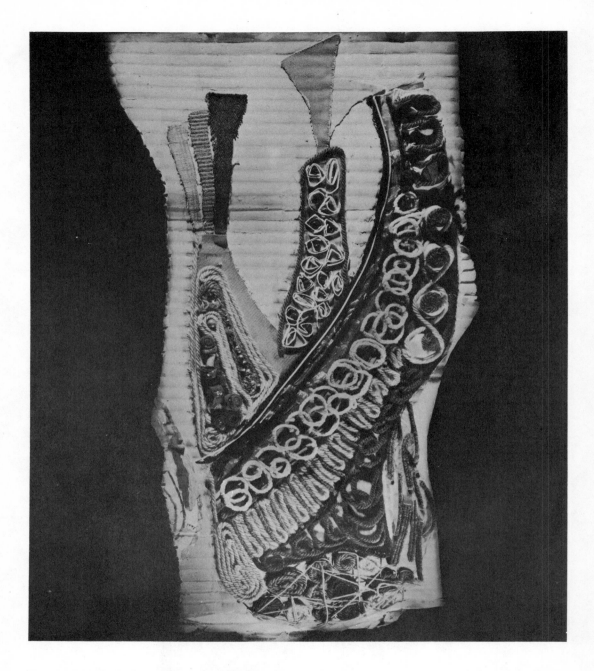

Section of a large collage by Helena McKinnon. Design inspired
by a celery head. Materials include wool, raffia, pipe cleaners,
sections of egg boxes, felt coils, wood, carpet offcuts and beads

54

make a fascinating pattern. When viewed from different directions, the effect of light shining on these surfaces will change and consequently form new shadows. By using transparent materials, such as acetate, you will achieve the added effect of seeing other colors and shapes, and with highly mirrored surfaces, such as Mylar, highly shiny areas and exciting reflections will be obtained.

Develop this idea by cutting and slotting in pieces of paper or card of various sizes, or partially cutting away sections of the background paper, bending the flaps outwards at varying angles so that they create interesting shadows on the background.

Highly reflective and matt papers used in forming the flat pattern and applied cylinders

Experiment with other shapes such as cubes, rectangles, sections of egg-boxes and molds. Cut holes of varying shape and size in some surfaces so that you gain even more views by looking through tunnels and into inner chambers. Some of these surfaces can be decorated. As constructions like these have a background, they are not, of course, free standing. However, this form of relief sculpture can be the first step towards delving into the problems and excitement of building models that can be viewed from all angles, or are, in other words, three-dimensional.

Basic patterns assembled from sections of egg boxes and enriched with plastic beads, sequins, felt strips and thread

Pattern made from sections of various types of egg box, with some shapes cut away and others inserted—sprayed with silver paint and decorated with aluminium foil and large sequins

'JUNK' MODELLING
(Three-Dimensional Work)

Materials needed:

Boxes, empty food containers, cartons, plastic beads, molds, cardboard rolls, empty canisters, wire, cellophane tape, scissors, white casein glue, staples, paint, collection of colored papers.

'Silver Creature' assembled from egg boxes—sprayed with silver paint and decorated with paper that has been cut and slotted, silver Mylar and beads

You can easily create three-dimensional models out of materials collected at home or at school. However, when making these free standing models, always remember to consider carefully all angles.

By assembling together cartons and boxes of varying size and trying them next to each other in a number of positions, you might see a resemblance to a strange object, animal or figure. Perhaps you can imagine a knobbly backbone, large staring eyes, the head and body of a weird creature or insect, part of a building or machine or some other feature that will form the basis of your model. Join the shapes together with glue, staples or cellophane tape

'Spiky Monster' by Peter Bennet—9 years. Made from egg boxes, a box with nails, paint tube tops, milk bottle tops, straws, assorted pasta, wood shavings, slotted card shapes and wool

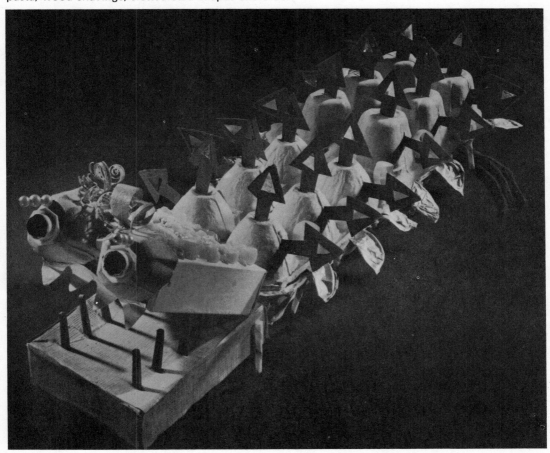

to make a more permanent fixture. When the main shape has been assembled, you could attach or slot small units at various angles to build the model into a more intriguing shape; remember that any structure is made more interesting by adding either large or small shapes. At this stage, it is quite a good idea to paint or spray all the sections to give a more unified appearance, as so often the containers used will be brightly labelled or marked by the manufacturer and these do not always enhance the work. Try to be original with final decorations or, if necessary, refer to previous sections. For instance, some of the cut paper patterns that were coiled, rolled, pleated or curled may add to the general effect.

Limit your color and allow the range of shapes and textures to enrich the model. You may like to add whiskers, hair, limbs, feathers, curls, lumps or other weird projections, but only if you honestly feel the assembly will benefit. Colored papers, beads and smaller details can be added if you want an encrusted surface. So many fascinating three-dimensional models are spoilt by not being sufficiently developed or decorated.

Finally, it should be repeated that the most important point to remember is to look very carefully indeed at your model from all angles to make sure that each view pleases you.

PHOTOGRAPHING FINISHED ARTWORK

Those of you with some knowledge of photography can have great fun photographing your finished collage work.

Many inexpensive cameras will produce a sharp image at a distance of 3 feet from the subject, enabling you to copy artwork of roughly 22×30 ins. For photographing smaller work, however, you will need to move nearer than 3 feet. In this instance a 'close up' attachment should be fitted over the camera lens, but it must be remembered that at close camera distances what is seen in the viewfinder will not correspond to what is recorded by the lens. This 'parallax error', as it is called, can be overcome by firstly framing your subject in the viewfinder and then moving the camera upwards by the distance between the lens and the viewfinder. This is most easily carried out on a tripod with a sliding centre column. The alternative is to use a 35 mm. single-lens reflex, where the viewfinder image is always identical to what is recorded on film, but this is much more expensive.

Most inexpensive cameras only have one or two relatively slow shutter speeds, so the use of a tripod is recommended with the camera set up parallel to the artwork.

If your collage is behind glass, try to avoid reflections by placing a large sheet of black paper between the camera and the subject, cutting a small circle for the lens to poke through. If your work is in a deep frame, avoid shadows cast by the frame.

For copying outdoors, dull light or hazy sun is best. The subject may be placed oblique to rays of direct sunlight for textural effect. If photographing indoors, use two photofloods equal distance from, and at about a 45° angle to, the artwork.

When copying in black and white and using a 'Weston' exposure meter, you can arrive at the correct exposure by taking a reading off a piece of white card held in front of the copy and placing the '0' setting on the dial against that reading. When copying in color, take a reading of the lighter parts of the subject and use the arrow setting. Because color transparency film needs accurate exposure, unless there is a permanent copy arrangement it is wise to expose three frames of film—one on the arrow setting, one giving $\frac{2}{3}$ stop more and one giving $\frac{2}{3}$ stop less.

CONCLUSION

The aim throughout this book has been to inspire and encourage you to create lively and original collage pictures and to gain experience of, and enjoyment from, using a vast range of exciting materials. It is also hoped that your powers of observation will have improved, so that you are able to appreciate more fully the intensely interesting scenes and details that surround you in everyday life.

Collage can certainly be regarded as an exciting art form in its own right; and you will probably enjoy looking for examples of this work, created by professional artists, that adorn hotels, restaurants, public buildings and shop windows in many towns and cities throughout the world.

Collage by Jean Baker—one of a series of Welsh panels for the Top Rank Ballroom, Cardiff

USEFUL BOOKS

	Published by:
The Young Embroiderer Jan Beaney	Frederick Warne & Co. Inc.
Designing with String Mary Seyd	Watson-Guptil
How to Make Collages Lynch	Studio/Viking
Collage and Found Art Meilach and Ten Hoor	Reinhold
Embroidery Stitches Anne Butler	Praeger
Adventures in Paper Modelling Payne	Frederick Warne & Co.
Creating in Collage D'Arbeloff and Yates	Watson-Guptil
Collage and Construction Harvey Weiss	Young Scott Books